I

I

I is born

By Arnaud Saint-Paul

Through this manifesto, Arnaud invites us to explore the depth of what it is to be *I* in this life and open one's heart to new possibilities such as finding harmony within.

Not only does he suggest a new framework of understanding but also a guideline to live our day-to-day through one's heart.

Living between New York and Paris, Arnaud went through his awakening when 13. He has been traveling throughout the world to study the different religions and philosophies in his relentless quest to understand himself. His life purpose is now to open billions of hearts and help them find harmony inside and out.

arnaudsaintpaul.com

Royalties of this book are donated to GIVE Nation 501(c)3, helping our children to become philanthropists and practice sustainable financial literacy (givenation.world)

Published by Tapuat Publishing

Printed in the United States of America

ISBN: 978-1-937296-09-4

Published date: 01/16/2025

TABLE OF CONTENT

For my kids, Jade and Sean

PREFACE

L ife! Our life can be amazing, sad, filled with wonders or ...stress. In our modern society, we could characterize it as a bit tumultuous ...most of the time. Most of us continue endlessly pursuing the trepidatious rhythm of life's hamster wheel, fearing to forego another experience, another event, or item that will fulfill for certain my craving... even if we don't know any more what needs to be satisfied!

Can our life be just summarized by this constant ebb and flow of drama and joyful moments? Should we choose for it to be just that or bring some meaning to that flow? When we look back, can we find some hidden coherence in the series of events that makes our past?

What would be the purpose of this life if not to figure out who we are? To experience and assess so many aspects of ourselves so that we can learn, step by step, moment after moment, who we want to become and adjust accordingly?

What if life, as it is, with its wonders and imperfections, is a way for us to decipher our innermost codes?

Each of us does it in a unique way of course: whether getting enthralled in business stories, or pressured by social conventions or passionate about raising kids, about music or art in general, climate change, ... The palette of colors from which we can each draw is infinite (and rightly so) so that we can paint the most perfect outcome we can imagine.

Most of the time though, like a ball in a pinball, we spend our lives jumping from one emotion to another, one thought to the next, getting, as time goes by, dispersed. Like on automated-pilot, we go through the hoops of life while feeling "out of tune" with ourselves.

Gradually, attracted by all the activities, we lose sight of our own presence, the one we are born with. Even if unconsciously aware, we develop a sense of permanent dissatisfaction. One that leaves an inexplicable feeling of emptiness tainting every day's experience with its somber tones.

That emptiness that we may choose to accept as part of our experience is the space from which we can, at last, envision what would look like another version of ourselves where "disorder" becomes coherence, where this "unruly" day-to-day finds its articulate expression.

In other words, if each event, emotion, thought, would be a series of notes that constitutes the music of our life, what would it be like to experience Cacophony (aka. "apparent disorder") versus Harmony (aka. coherence)?

Each of us goes throughout life, looking for more clarity, more definition, more love. Some constantly seek the Holy Grail that will save them, others just go through life's hoops, unconsciously. In any case, we all are looking for increased harmony whether we can find it within ourselves or outside.

Today's society offers us multiple ways to fulfill such need, starting with the ephemeral completion of our desires. Such completion that we construe as a moment of happiness is in its essence, deep down, our inner symphony seeking further coherence or harmony, so that it "plays out" a higher version of itself.

Harmony, though, could be understood as a vain word that does not apply to our frantic day-to-day where one needs to go to work, drive a car, fetch the kids, attend an event, answer calls, send emails, let alone spend more time with a loved one.

"'Harmony' whether inside me or with the rest of the world does not cut it", would you say.

And you would be right!

That is if we limit ourselves within the tiny scope of our human perception limited to our five senses and experience!

However, it could not be further from the truth when we go beyond that scope. What sciences of old such as Yoga, the science of Union, and modern ones such as Quantum Physics teach us about the world we live in, is that there is much more to what meets the eye. According to these sciences, what happens beyond our five senses and our limited perception of time and space has a huge impact on our daily life and how what we call reality unfolds. If you add to that the unconscious mechanisms at play whether they are physical (your different organs providing you with a healthy living), emotional (stuck emotions from a distant past), mental (thought patterns on auto-pilot), you have an amazing unconscious cocktail of hidden perceptions. Our conscious perception of our daily life is beheld by our subconscious and surrounded by our reality. Both seem, from our standpoint, to be immeasurably bigger. In other words, our conscious life is a bit like the crust of the Earth compared with its size: a super thin layer of natural miracle surrounded by unfathomable depths on both sides!

Fruit of 40 years of personal inquiry, the texts you are going to discover throughout these pages have been instrumental to help me on my journey towards myself understand some simple truths. They have helped me explore and expand my "conscious crust" so to speak. These truths, when applied, have been consistently helping me become a better person in all areas of what turned out to be, on all account, a thriving life.

They have led me to a state of harmony that was unveiled to me as I went writing these words while life was impacting me, in unison, like polishing a rough diamond, layer after layer.

Each of these lines however uses one core foundational assumption so that they become active and bring you the benefits it has brought so far to my life and so many readers'. This new foundation is here to help you reframe your understanding of your world and how you may choose to relate to it differently while reading these lines.

In other words, it is crucial that you understand how important this axiom is to impact your life should you choose to invite more coherence (aka. Harmony) as your core daily experience from now on.

This principle has the power to rock your world from top to bottom... in a very good way of course.

So, without further ado, here it is:

The world around you, all its manifestation (all the people, situations, events, moments), the one inside you (your body, your emotions, your thoughts), and within you (your presence) whether conscious or unconscious. All that (no exception) is made of

...

...

...

vibrations.

In other words, this world of form you are witnessing, touching, sensing, feeling, exists in its original state as vibration. That is to say, our perception mechanisms interpret vibrations to create for us a construct we name "reality".

If all that is (around and inside me) is made of vibrations, our life is very much like a set of notes on a musical score. Each of our organs, thoughts, emotions (past, present, future), situations, conversations, etc. are a series of vibrating notes. Each of them are superposed, sounding with their unique tune an aspect of what it is to be the wonderful you that you are.

Each resonating with each other, sometimes even mirroring one another, intertwining a multitude of threads that creates our experience.

Together, they compose a wondrous symphony that we call "our life".

Like any piece of music, this life-symphony of ours is constantly seeking its own coherence and harmony.

All its parts we mentioned earlier are a succession of overlapping patterns, each swirling with each other in their own tempo but at the same time looking to reach a certain degree of coherence with the rest of the symphony to create harmony. As the overall system finds its ultimate expression in such balance, any underlying pattern (aka. An organ, situation, thought, ...) may sound offkey for a little while, until it finds its new coherence within the whole. Once a pattern finds a new expression, it spreads itself out creating a new resonance throughout the whole, merging with it vibrationally.

This dynamic view of creation and our reality changes the very foundation of the way we understand and relate to ourselves. We let go of the illusory static image of ourselves (a particle separated from other particles), to get into a flowing and interdependent system of countless waves intertwined together, forming a coherent whole.

Once we adopt that understanding, everything becomes much simpler.

Every aspect of our life from illnesses, to events, from the influence of past generations on our present experience to past trauma in our childhood, from a project failure to a thriving business, comes to be self-evident: by accepting that new framework, that new lens through which we can view and experience our day-to-day life, we understand that every single interaction, thought, emotion, event are interwoven 'strings', resonating with each other, in an infinite musical portrait.

Suddenly, every concept we had about our life as an "independent particle or human", concepts based on difference, separation, struggle, survival, become irrelevant. Thus, we understand that all and everything is interdependent, from the smallest grain of sand on a beach in Tokyo, Japan, to the latest situation in our life, from a thought repeating itself in our mind to series of events that are directly related to it, from some past emotional trauma to a chronic illness.

All is interconnected.

As such, by changing our paradigm or framework, we open new pathways whereby, by tweaking the way we think, experience life, and live it, we start to feel that we are part of our surroundings, a bit like the drop in the ocean, that is also part of the wave, is rushing to the shore. We, therefore, surf the wave of life, feeling supported, being one of the instruments in such a big orchestra, composing, all together, this amazing composition that is our "life"!

As you can see, the new paradigm then applies to promote openness, collaboration, and abundance-based belief systems. Ones that seek further alignment, resonance, and coherence.

As a matter of fact, as the coherence rule that we explored earlier dictates, these are exactly the concepts called for by today's world's dire circumstances! Not a coincidence of course.

To recap, we now know that our very essence and the one of our reality is vibration-based (instead of the illusion of being a separated independent entity).

We also realize that what we call *I*, and the reality surrounding it, is therefore completely part of the whole creation, matching perfectly its surrounding like an Olympic surfer riding a mighty wave in Hawaii, communing, being One, with it.

Lastly, if all these vibrations are interdependent and part of a whole (aka. Your Life's symphony), that also means that *I* can shift its thoughts and emotional patterns and therefore 'upgrade' to a new vibration that will spread across the whole, thus creating a new set of vibrations and experiences.

In other words, we now understand that *I* has always the potential choice to whether continue on the same vibration patterns or select new ones which will, in turn, create a new set of experiences (and situations) from which it can choose again.

Therefore, by starting imagining a new world for yourself through the content of this book, you may open your heart to a self-actualizing "life" symphony that is always seeking its perfect alignment towards higher octaves (aka. More prosperity, health, and love). In other words, your life becomes more fulfilled, prosperous, and joyful.

Our only job is to listen...intently!

Written from a place of Harmony or higher vibrational frequency, the words you are going to discover will help you understand how harmony could pervade and (eventually) manifest in your daily life. They also may, if you allow it, help you experience what it means to have a harmonious life.

It would thus bring you many happy outcomes starting with a peaceful and joyful sense of Presence, being part of the flow.

Such effect will only unravel when a permanent feeling of gratitude, of "being part of the whole", takes hold. As you move further on that path, you may start feeling supported all the time, in all your endeavors.

Are you ready for such a life? Yes? Let's begin and learn how your life can become like an inspiring symphony every day, every moment.

Coming from a higher understanding of what our life could be and become, may these words open doors in your life and fulfill your dreams.

You will find below 66 odes or poems redefining core aspects of our lives. These poems are aimed to bypass the mind seeking knowledge so that you can feel (instead of learning) your path towards harmony.

They have helped me and countless clients gracefully better perceive how to be the best version of ourselves, day after day. You can read all of them and then pick a few to reflect on each concept.

You can also randomly pick one, live applying its principles for the whole day, and then feel how it changed you.

NEW ALCHEMY

New

New alchemy
New me
New way
Untried path
Leading away
From a renowned earth
To a space of me
That awaits myself to be

To be in that new normal
Is to choose now anew
Make it so formal
That now it is not so new

And on goes the wheel
The wheel of creation
The dance of the will

Now is the time
To step in your creation
Now is the time

When I is going through the same patterns, repetitively, what does a new normal look like? When does this change happen if not now?

Buoyancy

Marveled by the observed
Grateful for what is
Feeling the energy of what is
Being the encumbered expression
Of the Moment

In this Present, allow
At the Moment, glow
Be present to all that is
Including the infinite energy at your disposal

Be the manifested innocence
Be all that you can be
Now

Entrained by the importance of our day-to-day, we forget the gifts available to us such as, for instance, the energy of buoyancy.

Assertiveness

Step after step goes the *I*
Exploring its reflection throughout dimensions

Without a doubt
Without hesitation, No judgment
I chooses
I steps in, all of it, all it is

In that chosen dimension
From that new moment and place
I am
I am all that I am
The Alpha & Omega of this new world
That is Me

This independent world of Me
Free of all Ties
Is True to Itself
That new truth is to be explored
Step by step
In all splendor of the *I*

On its journey towards itself, I *needs to include some qualities like 'Assertiveness' if it wants to succeed in its endeavor.*

Trust

Amidst the apparent, I find
Amongst the unclear, I can see
Even through the walls of uncertainty
I step in, clearly, doubt-free
To the fulfillment of my dreams

I knows what is to be
With such certainty
It claims its realm of possibility
It chooses clearly
And allows what can be

With confidence, I rejoice
With faith, I recall
What it was to be
The subject of my dream
Manifested

O *I*, move swiftly
To your heart's desire
It is awaiting for you
In the pinnacle of your dreams

Pillar of your journey towards yourself, Trust is to be found in every crevice of your experience and magnified to the fullest to free yourself from your self-imposed shackles.

Heart

Infinite Me,
Eternal Observer,
Unconditional Loving Self,
I am

I am all that IS
All that is to be
All that was
One and the same

I am the object of my dream
That I watch, see and dream
I am the seer
I am the watcher
Of who I believe to be
Letting go, through love,
Of the illusive self
The one I believe to be

I am
I am Infinite Love

Exploring what it means to be I *from the Self standpoint.*

Wisdom

Traveling towards itself
I discovers more of itself
Earns & recovers its divine image
From heart to mind
From mind to Heart

Transcending illusion
I reflects
Seeing beyond itself
I deflects
Sensing a deeper *I*
I is, beyond itself

Through the knowledge of It
I speaks words of guidance
Through the eye of the Other

Bear my words for they are
Words of truth
Beyond the chasm of reality
Directly from the Source of Love

The "Eye", the conduit to our heart, is also the I *through which one speaks to himself.*

Love

I embrace all that I am
I accept all that I can be
I allow for my flow to be

I trust all that is
I have faith in me
I sense my unique Truth
Of Unity

No one is new to me
Only reflections populate my dream
In that kaleidoscope of me
I feel, loved, to the brim

Through the transparent veil of my beliefs
I forego the conclusion of my dream
On the path of discovery of me
I discover who am I to be

No one is to love but me
Alpha, Omega, Love is one
Love loves Love...I am

Day in, day out, let's accept and allow these words to populate our daily life.

Being

A journey into the unknown
Waves of colors on my path
Washed away,
Tossed amongst the shores of my heart

I uncover the joy of being
Found in the bliss of such art

Traveling in the darkest realms
I see the light
Light in my dreamer's eye
Leading me toward marvels of the *I*

All that I see
All that I feel
Is a rhythm,
A glee

Two but one
As One is All
Two creates
Sacred perfection
A unique dance
In total connection

Such is heaven
For one can create
Should he be awake
A reflection of thy heart
In the eye of the Beloved

I can only float
Shore to shore
Across the waves
Until when "s/he" will be

Then a destination is to be set
Full speed ahead
To the shore of my heart
Harbor of my soul

A dance between Self and I, *a journey from shore to shore, to find himself back where he started but all the happier to have found him-Self.*

The process of Creation only exists in duality where contrast is needed to foster the illusion of segregation or difference. Hence the illusion of I *can arise and the one of the "Other" can too, to produce the reality we call "life".*

Truth

Beyond what seems to be
I knows
In that unique tone
Is the key

The key to its own unfoldment
The key to the discovery of a new reality

Resounding is the Truth in Eternity
Clear is the signal within Infinity
It is my heart which sings
The perfect balance of what is...to be

Listen, listen, intently
For that tone of truth
Is disguised under many layers
Find amidst the noise
The purity of you, of *I*

Follow the cape of you
Meet the unfoldment
To what has always been!

Seeking truth invites us to the depth of the meaning of what is around us beyond what is apparent. Only to discover that our ultimate truth was already there in the first place.

Arise

From the apparent unknown
I arises
From the elusive fog of beliefs
I arise.
From the chaotic version of itself,
I chooses, becomes and arises.

Towards its chosen vision
I arose
Into a clear path towards itself
I chose
To the completion of all it can be
I embraced, loved, rose

Step into your magnificence
Choose joy and majesty
Even with a tad of petulance
It is for you, at last, to be

Rejoice, enjoy, arise
Discover all that you are to be
For it is your gift to rise infinitely

*Part of I's journey is to start believing in itself and accept
that it can be more, that it deserves to be more too.*

Persistence

Round and Round
Is the path to oblivion
Lost in the sound
Of my beliefs in motion
I pray

Long is the journey
To fulfillment of my vision
Following without apprehension
My Truth

Amidst the illusive appearances
Follow Thy Heart
Follow Thy Vision

As you insist on that inner evidence
The Path will unfold
The new Normal is shown

Rejoice!
For you are treading the divine alley
Of your Choice

In its first steps, I stumbles and loses the path that it chose.
Persistence is key to enable the New Normal to take hold.

Liberty

Where do I go?
What focus to choose?
Out of the infinite possibilities
It is *I* which decides to be

Out of the chaos of what *I* could be
A certain shape already aligns
The basic principles of my Experience

It is up to me to transcend
Such apparent limitations
And discover to my bewilderment
The ease which is to be it

Long is the way to freedom
Short is the path to presence it
Allowing my Self to be part of it

Stepping decisively upon it
And resonate at last
With the music of my heart

As I *steps into its journey, possibilities abound.*

Serendipity

As *I* walks and discovers
Plucking away
The remanences of past dreams

Amidst the apparent chaos
An oasis appears as it seems
Surprising resonance,
Apparent miracle,

This new image of you/I
Shows what ought to be seen.

Ultimate sound of perfection
Conjured moment out of thin air
Expressing a unique step to completion
A magical stride, pure and fair.

Wondrous truth revealed
Moment of utter harmony
Until the next one, concealed,
In the journey to your Dream

According to the dictionary, "Serendipity" means 'the occurrence and development of events by chance in a happy or beneficial way'. What if it did not happen by 'chance' but by resonance?

Time

Crawling away from its womb
I is born
Segregated Self, moment to moment,
I gets torn... off itself

As the Father of all duality,
Mother of all steps,
Time brings solace
To thy journey towards *I*

From naught to infinite,
From love to Love,
Such are the steps to Nirvana

Blessed are the moments
Setting apart the experience of the Whole
So that *I* can find
The epitome of its dreams

For I *to exist Time is needed to provide the journey's experience of evolution and change*

Faith

Touching the reality around me
I watch
Addicting dance with what seems to be
I play

Powerful is the illusion
To obliterate the vision
Replacing what ought to be
By the heart of my Truth to be

Do not dangle
Do not sway
For beyond what is
Is what is to be

Follow the sparkle of Truth
That lies in your Heart
Blind your eyes and go
Follow your dream

As in every moment lies
The manifestation of your faith

I *needs Faith in oneself to transcend what* I *calls its reality.*

Certainty

In the flow of life, *I* knows
Among the turbulence of doubts
I chooses

Without clear evidence
With no signs ahead
I closes its eyes
Seeking its truth... inside

Manifest is the path
Obvious is the vision
No doubts to cloud what is
A marching order towards inevitability

Amidst the apparent muddiness
I advances
Losing sight of its current reflection
I steps forward
To the fulfillment of its inner vision
With sureness and poise

In the constant fog of life, I can muster its will to open its path beyond what is shown.

Sureness

Will I?
I will
Forceful journey
Towards new beginnings

Marching away
With strength and joyful happening
Resolute steps
To envisioned shores
No doubts to be heard
As it is the Creator's will!

To each ask
A resolute "yes!"
Is manifested across all dimensions

To revere Thy Self
In its resounding glory
With joy and recognition!

'Sureness' complements 'Certainty', strengthening I's *journey towards its Self.*

Surrender

Willful *I*
Driven by the effect
Swollen by the illusion
Of Its reflection

Perceptual *I*
Tuning into
The surrounding flow
Of the inner cause

Allowing *I*
Giving in
To the relentless whisper
Of inner guidance

Surrendering *I*
Carried away
Of his own veil
To the fulfillment
Of his inmost Dreams

For I to shed its own 'skin', surrendering is a stepping stone towards being reborn to itself...

Compassion

Gentle *I*
Witnessing life's flow
Encompassing all that is
And could be
And grow

Open thy arms and heart
For it is thy mission
To embrace all
That is shown to you
As it is part of your Self
And thus, is waiting,
For your love
And attention.

Now is the time
To let go of all prejudice
And accept all that you can be
In this infinite wheel
Of a lifetime

...with 'Compassion' towards all that is around I and most importantly itself!

Freedom

Birds in the sky
Wings in heaven
Heading away
Rising to the Sun,
All knowing Source
Of Light.

No shackles, no bonds
Just the knowledge
Of whom I am to be
And then let go
Of whom I believed to be

Unfettered, *I* is born
Unbound, chooses to be
Expanding its wings
With sureness and confidence
To experience the new seed
Of its own Self

In 'Freedom', I is born and to Freedom, it shall return.
Should it choose to do so.

Grace

Synchrony
Harmony
In Infinity
Eternal congruity of the *I*

From dissonance
Of the multiplicity
To resonance
Of Unity

Finding the Pathway
Unstoppable dance
Joining the way
Of the perfect Balance

Dual energy,
Faithful steps, following,
The Outer Dream

No questions, no doubts,
Just the Choreography of my Dream

To be in the flow of life, I is to accept itself and find its own resonance to be "in tune".

Life

Tic toc
Time passing by

Flic floc
Moments after Moments
Learning to fly

Joyful steps of discovery
Into one's heart
Carried by the wings of my dreams

One leap at a time
Climbing my way in rhyme
I surrender to thy beauty
I yield tutti

Lead the way
Mold thy clay
So that I can be
The best expression of Thy Love

Mindful invitation of I *to its Self to go through 'Life' in coherence /resonance with it.*

Sweetness

Fleeting moment
A caress in the sky
Pink movement
Remembrance in my mind's eye

Sensual travel
As the present unravel
Beautiful treasure
Unfold for my private pleasure

Untold stories
Of love and glories
Sweet touch
Delightful penuche

Graceful life
Glorious wife
Indubious expression
Of Thy Ascension

Life's journey can include many types of experiences. Which type of experience shall I invite to this Now moment?

Pronoia

Constant support
Continuous nurturing
Growing love
By a benevolent universe

Hard to believe
I avoids the truth
Scared to be relieved
Of its sacred duty

Let go of your fears
Accept to be in the flow
Allow to be surprised
Open up to constant reception

For it is your divine right
Your natural path
To be adored
My Beloved

What do I choose as my current default state? Paranoia or Pronoia?

Abundance

Infinite possibility
Eternal choices and experiences
No limit to what can be
But the focus of my *I*

Where to look?
When to sway?
All potentials at my service
For me to select where my *I* should lay

Expand
Rejoice
All that *I* want to be
I can experience

For it is the very reason
Of each unique moment
Magnificent dance
Of endless love

*Letting go of the 'particle' I implies surrendering the notion
of scarcity and accept, and allow, abundance to be I's
default life experience.*

Joyful

Free of all concerns
I play
Expecting constant support
I laugh

No doubts, no questions,
One rule only applies
Expressing One's life
In joy, happy!

Let the Universe care
Allow yourself to be free
For your Path is alight
With brilliance everywhere

Leave the shore of seriousness
Bring about the sea of joy
In each and every moment is the key
To your best expression of joy and happiness

For this is your nature,
This is who you are

No journey towards Self can he had without the adoption of joyfulness to be applied to every single moment of our life.

Serenity

Poise,
Grace,
Such is the Pace

One step
Another
All in due time
No rush

Easy is the Path
To the Inner Vision
Certain, the way
To Completion

Glowing moment,
Open arms,
To the fulfillment
Of my dreams

No doubts,
But bliss,
In the unfoldment of Me

*I can only find its Self in that space where 'Serenity' and
'Peace' glide together...*

Peace

Eternal Mirror
Perfect Reflection
No stir, no vision,
No error

Unfathomable
But so true
Pure expression
Of Love

Clear balance
Flawless image
Of my Self

Pure moment
For me
To Be

Infinite perception
Of all that I am

...as it gets lost in its own... image.

I am

I
Center of all that is
I
Mirroring what is to be

Director of all circumstances
Reflection of my Dreams
False attempts to be Me
On the true Path to my Truth

Infinite maze of possibilities
Constant rebirth into expansion
I chooses to be
All that it can be

Now is the time
To choose what I am to be
And live all that I am
In this infinite moment of my Dream

From the Self to the I, *from* I *to Self, what is to be who I am?*

Illusion

Apparent vision
Of an elusive reality
So clear reflection
Of who I believe to be

Object of transcendence
Absolute contrast
Conventions to blast
Away from present stance

But do not forget
That in that *I* to be
Is the seed I bet
On to become who I am to be

Such is the illusion
Pathway to my oblivion
Source of the fusion
To my Dream

I *only exists within the belief that the contrast it observes, reality, is tangible.*

Positivity

Out of all that is
A choice
Limiting or,
Expanding.
Fear or,
Love.
Negative or,
Positive.

Ride, ride the wave
The wave that lifts *I*
In a never-ending spiral
Of goodness

Stride with faith
Trust your steps
Choose with discernment
The path to eternal growth

Now is the time to rebirth
In your positive *I*

I *always choose negative or positive thoughts, actions, emotions. This in turn enables a series of experiences that are a direct consequence of such a choice in the next moment.*

Ego

Layer after layer
Reversed perception of *I*
Unclear vision
Shaping who *I* believes to be

Veil to all that *I* could be
Contrast to whom *I* wants to be
Serving a purpose towards a vision
Of who *I* is bound to be

Such is the ebb and flow
Reflection of what it is to become
Layer after layer
Unveiling *I*
In the depth of thy thoughts

Now is the time
To be all that *I* can be
Now is the only moment
To transcend into divinity

Shedding away the infinite layers that I *has carefully left in the Past or Future to find its Self, Now.*

Growth

Out of duality
Illusion of movement
Exploration of the *I*
Mighty swing of what could be

Expansion, contraction
Ebb and flow
Such is the Dance
Where I sough

So many dimensions
Of one's own vision
Discovery of *I*
Letting *I* die

Rebirth, joy and truth
Here is the new *I*
In its magnificent youth
Ready to uncover
Its new reality

Within the duality of this life, I *explores and discovers its Path towards its own Unity, the one it is already part of.*

Joy

Eternal Fountain
Abyssal Well
Deep expression of me

Before Creation,
Limitless lake.
Reflecting the *I*
Infinite manifestation
Of all that *I* could be

I drinks to the Chalice
Jug of delight
Pure expression
Of all that *I* can be

In that infinite moment
Of Now
Seize it!
And express
All that you are to be

From a Self perspective, from that fountain of pure Joy,
Self invites I to dwell in it and live through it.

Confidence

Surrounded by reflections
Apparently lost in these visions
Find its center
I must

I focus
I transcend
Beyond the apparent
I manifest

For there is no resistance
To the existence
Of my Truth

As I am living it
Now
Amidst the shadows of my dreams

Spear ahead
Trust your heart
And you shall reap
The fruits of what seems

Finding its true center in the Now moment, I *chooses its Path in pure alignment with itself.*

Presence

Scattered amongst shadows
I exist
Forgotten core
Across the shores
I find

Past, present, future
Illusive stories
The only time is
Now

Still is thy peace
Joyful is thy Bliss
All that can be
Is
All that I want to be
Can be

Amidst the change
Among the flow
I is, eternal presence of itself

In this Now Moment is the Presence of I *shall* I *choose to presence it.*

Receive

Strangled *I*
Frozen into shape
Victim of its own rape
I stumbles in its nigh'

There is the evergreen flow
Carrying away cry and woe
Source of so many riches
A choice is made, *I* unhitches

Sailing away
Releasing its own way
Of being, *I* melds

Opening its heart
Allowing, running like a hart
In love, *I* welds

Allowing oneself to receive is an important step towards opening up to life's bounties. Hence, letting go of one's strong belief in duality and therefore in its particle/tangible state is the first stride towards effortless support.

FROM *I* TO SELF

Birth

I is born
Mother

Seeking your I
Beacon of Light
Wondrous connection
Mesmerizing apparition
Getting closer to you
Searching for the perfection
That makes it you
Pure love expressed
In this mundane world
You helped me find my way
Through the love-beat of your Heart

Tic Toc
Your Love calls

Tic Toc
I arises

Tic Toc
Now is the time

Tic Toc
To enter the fray

Nurtured, loved, supported
I goes astray
To discover itself

Loved, nurtured, supported
I finds its way
To a world of bliss

Mother, from the deepest bottom of my heart
Thank you
For letting me come about, Thank you
For all the sacrifices you made, Thank you
For all the love you mustered, Thank you
You are my beacon of light

To you, with gratitude, I bow
I kneel
I kiss
I thank thee
For all the gifts you bestowed upon me

Mother, I love you
For all eternity,
Unconditionally

Prior to our physical birth, the journey has already started where consciousness gradually come and becomes, called by Love, a self-identified being.

Journey

In this mire of ourselves,
I find its way towards itSelf
A journey of cries and woes
Changing along its weaving path

Moment to moment
Thought to thought
The illusion of *I* perpetuates
Through these, *I* exists,
Moments of contrast against a backdrop of infinity

Alike these lines on the white paper
The black swirl of these thoughts
Imprint their patterns
Upon the never-ending potentials of life

Moment after Moment
Thought after Thought
I live, and believe, to be who I am.

With Presence as the background, our experience is enacted through the eyes of our I *to deliver to us the life we love so much.*

To thy Heart

Your light is so bright
That with all my might
I did, do, will fight
For it to remain such sight.

So dark can be the soul
When one can be such a fool
As to forget One's sole
Purpose: not to control
But to get out of the rabbit hole.

So bright is the sight
Of one's true Self
That no army can fight
But only to plight oneself

Limitless is your Love
Infinite is your Light
Please my dove
Radiate and light the night

Of so many darkened souls
As they are seeking without respite
Without knowing, as wise fools,
That which is to ignite
Their endless thirst to Be.

Please I pray Thee
Reborn from your ashes
Be the Phoenix who dashes
With such mighty force
That no shadow can alter its course.

Love is your birth name
Compassion your game
Let us enjoy their Light
Through which You shall indite.

Between the I *and the Self, between Mind and Heart, a
dialog exists. One made of uniting and mesmerizing love
on* I*'s journey towards its higher expression.*

Love

Love is the key
Love is the key, the hole, the door,
Love pervades all
The key is in the *I*
I which isolates from Love
Eye which does not See
Love Is
While *I* does
Love invites *I* into oneself
For its eternal Joy.

I *(note the word-play between* I *and "Eye") represents the Ego, the identification to its body and its reality. The Heart, representing Beingness, and the Ego, representing Doingness, speak to one another.*

Know thyself

Know thyself
Love thyself
Experience one's depth
Beyond a thought
Beyond the mind
In the midst of who I am
Uncovering joyousness again
Deep and permanent

Pure joy, true joy, perspiring shallow constructions,
Structures that cannot withstand such blissfulness
Bodies aligning with loving simplicity.

Grace, harmony, the art of serendipity,
Beauty, symphony, permanent synchronicity
No end to the game, no border
Perpetual expansion into one another

Ever and ever, thriving into one's heart
To provide for what is, now.

Love is the key,
To one's reality
As worry
Is none but from duality

I do not want to forget
Even entangled in drama
What heart is *I*
What Joy is NOW

Eternal giving
Infinite offering
No limit, no border
LOVE

Love exists within whichever the I, *the Ego's doing, creating its own drama. Within the Now moment, is the pure, untainted joyfulness of one's reality.*

Song to my Twin Flame

Dear beloved
You are One
One with Me

Get into my bliss
As I will care for you
Forever. As you are One,
One with Me

Let me sing to you
Song of ever ending
Love
Let me sing for you
Joyous song of You

You, incarnated
You, being
You, total heart

I totally accept You
You are Me and I, You

Let's sing together
Let's dance together
The song-dance of life
For I will care for me/you
In all eternity

Welcome to yourself
Welcome to your dream
Your dream come true
In all reality

For I-we am-are the Tune
Where-when all tones are manifested
And can surrender to
And be loved in each moment.

For I love you
And you love I

*On our journey towards ourselves, the world, our partner,
becomes a pure reflection of ourselves, helping us deepen
our love beyond the apparent.*

Free of me

Bright is the day
And I will go astray,
Follow my whims
Until light dims

Going with my heart
Straight like a dart
Without a thought
Out of any doubt

I see landscapes
I gape at such sea
That my heart escapes
And run, with glee

I laugh, flying like a dove
For I am Love
And Love is me.

Beyond what is shown in our reality, we always have the choice of being grateful and see the freedom provided to us. As a consequence, more often than not, more freedom and reasons to be grateful show up in our life.

I

I
Eternal Bliss
Infinite Love
Timeless Creation

Now, you will find
Me. In freedom, I thrive
In passion, we share
The endless dance of life

Into Awareness, I am
Without past, present, future
Dive into me
Be alive
Lead by my hand
Like having a wand
Live your dreams
Uncover your wishes
Be wild, be bold
For there is no limit
But the ones you define

Discover new dimensions
Walk past illusions

There you will find me
In the middle of nowhere / no when
In the midst of your heart.

I, *in this poem, personifies one's Heart, or Higher Self,*
Love, speaking to me from across one's Ego self.

From *I* to self

Love unites

Love
Such a grace
Silence
Such a deafening sound

I play by your silence
Listen to my music
Such harmony that your love
Brings, lightening my Path.

O heart, nest of such beauty,
I shan't bear the thought
Of forgetting
But to pursue, aware,
This journey of infinite Love.

Angels pave my way
Wings give flight to my dreams
That I secretly wove
Into the fabric of my reality.

As sure as I am Love
I will meet thee
And explore again, love,
This dimension of Unity.

This is the key
To our next discovery
Where all differences melt
Into one sole joy we dwelt.

I hear your silence
I thank your love
I shall enjoy both
And transcend eternity

In response to the previous poem, I, *an enlightened Ego, answers.*

Wind in the air

Wind in the air
Wings into my hair
A seagull flying in the light
Love, at first sight

Air, sand, sea,
Simple essences to be
Being aware of me
Senses in the harmony

A bird play in the air
A point, me, in my lair,
Two beholders, one below, the other, above

Transcending the illusion
One heart, one dimension,
Into an ocean of Love.

For Self and I *to meet,*
It can only happen in the Present beat
In the simplicity of this moment,
Enabling now, its atonement.

Love, birthing its wings

Love, birthing its wings
Flapping, trying
To fly.
A glitter in the eye.

Shyly, unbelieving its beauty
Love uncovers himself
Lightening into serendipity
Growing anew into Self

A glow to which One bow
A blink, light as an arrow,
My world shifts, open.

I am loved, love is one,
Bathed in love, expand into One,
All creation is mine, my own den.

*Gradually the Ego discovers its own divinity, within Love,
and finds out that he is the sole point of origin of its world,
what we call 'reality'.*

Silence

Silence is the key
To uncover thee
No waves,
Just a plain... sea

Beyond description
A Lone perception

No way to see
But to perceive Thee
No words can describe
To which I abide

Such an infinite presence
Deep into my essence
I meet Thee, my Love
High in the sky above

Here, there, everywhere
You are present, in the air?
Across all that which is
I bath, loved, in your bliss

Across noises, physical perceptions, below thoughts, emotions, inner perceptions, beyond the eternal witness is Love, Presence, the Source, All That Is, God, ...

It is just a Dream

It is just a dream
Within a dream

Dream of light
No matter what
Dream of wrongs and Right
Illusion, mirrors, mystery

One sole truth
Honed to one
One sole path
Toward true life

Go through the waves
Fly through the nave
In your inner being
Lies your only destiny

Unveil the authentic cave
Where One beats with crave
Meet your own Heart
That which guides you like a dart

Sing, dance, chant your life
Listen to your music
No one can hear it
Only you can follow it

It will guide you through dimensions
Toward your own appreciation
Surrender to your Love
Love your surrender

See that nothing can miss
Unless guided by your own doubts
Seek your permanent bliss
Find the ideal whereabouts

Love your own creations
As they love you in all dimensions
Feel the pervading love around you
Shine the love within you

And you will find
In good time
That all
Is fine.

Beyond this 3D world, what if this reality was only a reflection, lighting up one aspect of Me? What if, beyond this mesmerizing world, surrender and love are the keys?

Blazing light

Blazing light
Soothing Sea
Eternal reflection of thee
Hollow mirror into thee

The sun beams
Onto the ocean stream
Startles the viewer
Wonders the observer

I, in awe, chooses not to be
I, subdued, uncovers the eternal flow
Bathed, surrendered, *I* is what it should be:
The permanent eye in the ever flow.

Thoughtful bliss
Overpowering hiss
I, wanders in the ever-ending spring
A guest, in the house of the gods.

A perception from the Divine of where the Ego (I) should stand.

A world of light

Imagine a world of light.
A world, full of prisms,
For your own delight.

One form to the next,
Each follows its text
All into your expansion.

None are but you
No difference, only you,
A grand game to be played
Actors forgotten to themselves!

Grand game of awareness
On a big board of chess,

One result, one end:
Grand expression of Love
Manifestation from above.

A world envisioned from the point of view of Love, of the Creator, who roams within his own reality among the multitude of mirrors that populates his world.

Creation Fly!

A few black words on white pages
Some notes flying around
So many worlds across the ages
Infinite perceptions to which One was bound

Slow is the rhythm, clear is the path,
Should One perceive it, in silence,
Not imposing his own beat
Not identifying to any projected tones

Let your Creation fly
Let it thrive
Make no noise, but poise,
Wait until it expresses itself,
To its full extent

And see again and again,
Love in every detail
Love it as it will love you
Be one and sublime in your bliss.

Within my inner silence, by letting go of the Do's and Must's (the identifications to my reality), by listening intently to my heart, I can begin to clearly view and more importantly feel the rhythm and path of my own Creation, in total alignment with myself, allowing her to guide me in her expansion... of love.

Gratitude

Wrapped in your arms, I pray
Surrounded by your love, I play
Charmed by your tone, I dance
Deep into your eyes, my proper stance

O divine Love,
I shan't be without You
For I, do not exist
But to Be, for You.

O divine Love,
I thank thee to be,
And experience bliss
Aware, in your presence.

O my divine Love,
My humble heart beats
For You and only You
Full of love and gratitude
To You, my source of bliss.

This poem of the I, *the personification of me within duality,
to Love, the Source, All That Is, plays also with the idea that
that Love is also personified by my Muse on Earth.*

Infinite mirror

O infinite mirror,
Magical reflection,
Without you I shall not be
In you, I can know me

O infinite echo
Of my own self,
You are my dream
You are my love

In the echo of my own reflection
Love adds to love,
Infinite loop of a divine dance
Wondrous symphony of one Heart.

As the sole creator of my reality, I *is reflected in the numerous mirrors enacted by my co-creators in this divine act.*

Pebble in a pond

A pebble in a pond
White spot in sea of gray
Infinite nuances of mist
Limitless borders of perception

One pebble in the pond
Pebble of potentials and joy
Light to the brim
In the midst of obscurity

The only pebble in the pond
Dreams of possible seas
Full of life, play, and joy.

All that is not the pebble
Strangled in their sleepy life
Yet to uncover their dream.

Yet, the only pebble in the pond
Will dance, play and sing,
To the sound of his love
For you.

The pebble here symbolizes individuality, the identification to one's reality that gives birth to the Ego/mind. This poem explores the contrasts between a self-aware consciousness and its co-creators ("All that is not pebble").

From: All That Is

Peace
Joy.
I am
Not what I thought/think.

One single being
From earth to sky and beyond

Formless, shapeless, directionless,
The eternal testimony of my own bliss
I am
I am in all forms, shapes and directions.
Without distinction, no identification.

From here to there
No space in between
Only Love that shapes the world inside

I am
I am love, only love,
Inside out, no border can be.
As there is nothing but love,
Sole expression of my essence.

Be what I am
No other truth
Only what you are, is
It is your only truth

Fray free in the stream of love
Free the sails, cross the veil,
And merge into Me

I am all
And nothing at all
I am me, he and thee,
I am the nutshell of all
And nothing beyond me

You, He, I, one and the same
Be content and play
For ever and ever
In love

Oh, how much I Love You

Love, the Divine, ... speaks and shares with us its perception of our play in this life.

Tree in my sight

Tree in my sight,
I Am, inside it.
People chatting, playing, musing,
All the same in me.

A play of my attention
Potential to identification.
Lost essence, plentiful minds,
A limited game of identification.

From birth, discovery of reality,
Objects of intention,
Away from the only reality.

Constant movement,
Eternal change,
Away from *I*
Far from Me

It is the second birth
That brings you back
To Me
Back from the shadows
Of ephemeral attention

Here,
Eternal stance
Of infinite love,
The most delicate vibration
Of your core dimension.

Stay, be and rejoice,
You are Home,
Which you never left,
For all eternity.

From the perspective of the Higher Self, that which IS, pure Being, Love, the identification process creates a separation, a segregation of consciousness that is then embodied by the mind/ego (and what we call the physical body): the I. *This* I, *this consciousness within duality, gradually "unpegs" itself from its identifications to find out that it is already ONE with itself.*

Spelled by such beauty

Spelled by such beauty
Enthralled by so much harmony
I walk and see All That Is, with glee

Pure reflection of my intention
I marvel at such glory
And only one answer comes to me:
Love the objects of my invention

Star Jewel of my crown,
Wondrous gift in my reality,
I bow to thee,
Goddess of my dreams

And love you,
Always,
In eternity.

From the perspective of I, *we explore its relationship with its reality and the people within it.*

Moments of love

Gentle breeze
Caresses thy skin
Of my divine be

Luminous day
Lights my way
To inner freedom

Disconnected from past
I sail, free, from my old
Self. A new beginning,
Lost in love,
Met with love,
At last, into my being.

Now
Is the time.
Set the sail
And fly
To your inner shore
In love.

Open up,
Let your borders go,
One sole direction:
Unlimited love toward
Your infinite reflection.

One mage, one muse,
One heart: a symphony
Of love, twirled in Love,
To become, in bliss.

My Heart to you,
Sing your song,
Play your tone,
And pledges itself
To you!

For the dispersed I, *a journey towards itself...following its Heart.*

Silence is golden

Silence is golden
Stillness in the heart

Gentle vibrations
Around my core,
Sweet manifestations,
That which I adore

One tone above all
Show me the way
To my inner doors

Such a bright light
I cannot go astray

Thank thee to be
Beautiful guide to me
Magnificent reflection
Of my eternal perfection

I can only meet you in love
And pray thee to be
Now and ever
In my reality

I love you, my me!

I *falling in Love with itself, with its Higher Self, with its reflection in its own reflection, in the eyes of his love.*

Journey across Me

Journey across me
Me as mere point in the whole
Me who is it all
And all nuances in between

Me, a singularity in the ether
Forget who is He
But believes what he is not
Spread amongst his own puppets

Out of the head of the pin,
The Ether. The wholeness
Of who I am, forgotten among
Human. In the ashes of the *I*
Lives the truth of what is Thy.

Objects of the *I*, I lie in the chasm
Of death. Death till the impending bly,
To Be all that I Am, no string
To what seems and that is not.

That all that I am, is what is,
And not one of these, I am only.
No quest for the inner grail
For I am all that is,

The grain and the light,
No frontier but freedom and bliss
Pin and wholeness, dark and light,
All that I am, I accept,
All that I am, I love,
All that I am, I fall in love with,
Eternally blessed.

No need to worry,
No need to be any
I am but me
That is the only to see.

I am here, now and present,
Enjoying the beautiful moment
Sacred presences in all that is
Handsome actors in their blessed moments.

Love is what I am
Love is what I shall be
Let love spray out
Let love brighten the way

I Am Me
I Am Love
I Love Me
I Love Thee

From the perspective of an enlightened I *on its path
towards more coherence and harmony.
Bly: Happy in Afrikaans.*

Letter from my Heart

What is seen
Has just been
Pure reflections
Of old intentions

Mix of new and old
The now, on hold.

The *I* changes:
From dry mental
To warm heart,
Back and forth,
The *I* blends.

Let Thy open,
Cuddle in my arms,
I will care
Of your 'broken' parts.

Let Thy thrive,
Become what you are,
As there is nothing
But all that is well.

In the silence of your heart
I am, to be,
Let me come afore
As this is your shore.

I am the walker,
Wonderful lover,
Now we shan't miss
Eternal bliss,

In Love.

Mere illustration of the enlightenment process when I *and Self start to merge together and become one.*

In time, Now is key

In Time: Now is key,
For, in this moment,
All Is and you can Be,
All potentials are here, dormant.

Explore, thrive, dance, play,
Be the joy within,
Light your way
Be the Unity herein.

For you–I are, untold,
The lighthouse of our dreams
Which, in time, unfold.

In Time is the key
To savor our dreams
And be, in them, with glee.

I Love You

Within the NOW moment, oblivious of pasts and futures, lays all the possibilities of one's life and an unfathomable depth of one's experience.

In the eons of time

In the eons of time
I have met You

In the deepest space,
Planets and galaxies,
You have shared with me

Every drop of time
Every manifestation
Is but a dream of You

One single note heard is a symphony
To your ageless beauty

Through the outer space
Every particle of my Universe
Sing to You

Every rock, every stone,
Every flower in this wondrous world,
Is a reflection of You

Marveled, I witness You
Across time, lives, dimensions, space,
My Beloved.

You are my Heart of Heart
You are my Bliss
You are my own sweet reflection
My world, my pearl.

Now, hands in hands,
We will roam the world
Enjoy all its treasures
And rejoice in the Creation
I have made
For You.

The I *found him-Self and now rejoices in unison and unity.*

Higher Self's dream

I dream,
I remember,
I see what has been, is and will be.

One single energy dream
Beam together in the emptiness
Dance, sing, rejoice, commune,
Free!

All is Now.

Infinite Love is the word
Word of which we are made of
I, You, others, mingled together
In a loving eternity.

O you, daring one,
Decide to go on the playground
To have fun one last time.

And shall we meet, let's say,
Here, then and there?
In That Now moment?

A little challenge?
Who will be the one regaining consciousness first?

Then the separation game begins
Consciousness dance to the smallest particle
Worlds are beheld, others created,
The game set is shaped

The actors enter the arena
What a wondrous symphony
Let's play and roam free
In Love.

The Higher Self, before coming into the lower planes (our reality), sets up some 'rendez-vous' with his half-'God spark'.
This poem is the introduction to a book that will be written a short while after: The Human Project (if you haven't read it go find it in the best online stores).

CONCLUSION

I am grateful for the fact that you have reached the end of this series.

As you can imagine, you can read this book straight or pick one text to refine one or several aspects of your life. Some of these poems revisit concepts behind keywords on which we base our lives, some share a taste of what it is to become more harmonious.

If you are looking to go deeper into any of the concepts explored in this book, we would be happy to have you join our community of Harmony-Livers (!) so that we can find together perfect coherence and alignment with our Heart.